Celebrating Differences

Different Appearances

by Rebecca Pettiford

Bullfrog Books

Ideas for Parents and Teachers

Bullfrog Books let children practice reading informational text at the earliest reading levels. Repetition, familiar words, and photo labels support early readers.

Before Reading

- Discuss the cover photo. What does it tell them?

- Look at the picture glossary together. Read and discuss the words.

Read the Book

- "Walk" through the book and look at the photos. Let the child ask questions. Point out the photo labels.

- Read the book to the child, or have him or her read independently.

After Reading

- Prompt the child to think more. Ask: Think about your best friend. How do you look different on the outside? What do you have in common on the inside?

Bullfrog Books are published by Jump!
5357 Penn Avenue South
Minneapolis, MN 55419
www.jumplibrary.com

Copyright © 2018 Jump! International copyright reserved in all countries. No part of this book may be reproduced in any form without written permission from the publisher.

Library of Congress Cataloging-in-Publication Data

Names: Pettiford, Rebecca, author.
Title: Different appearances / by Rebecca Pettiford.
Description: Minneapolis, MN: Jump!, Inc., [2017]
Series: Celebrating differences | Audience: Age 5-8.
Audience: K to grade 3. | Includes index.
Identifiers: LCCN 2016051871 (print)
LCCN 2017007012 (ebook) | ISBN 9781620316689
(hardcover: alk. paper) | ISBN 9781620317211 (pbk.)
ISBN 9781624965456 (ebook)
Subjects: LCSH:
Physical anthropology—Juvenile literature.
Human anatomy—Variation—Juvenile literature.
Classification: LCC GN62.8 .P46 2017 (print)
LCC GN62.8 (ebook) | DDC 599.9—dc23
LC record available at https://lccn.loc.gov/2016051871

Editor: Jenny Fretland VanVoorst
Book Designer: Leah Sanders
Photo Researcher: Leah Sanders

Photo Credits: Adobe Stock: javannig, 5. Alamy:
Ira Berger, 19. Getty: Flashpop, 1; charlie schuck,
6-7; Image Source, 8-9; Jose Luis Pelaez, 20-21;
iStock: monkeybusinessimages, cover; Nata_Snow,
11; Wavebreakmedia, 12-13, 14-15; DOUGBERRY,
16-17; valeriebarry, 18. Shutterstock: Andy Dean
Photography, 3; Brocreative, 4; Duplass, 10;
Hasnuddin, 22ml; ESB Professional, 22bm; Stuart
Monk, 22tl; Gelpi, 22tl, 22mr; Alan Sheldon, 22tr;
Valua Vitaly, 22bl; Rannachai Palas, 22br; Daxiao
Productions, 22tm; Nanette Grebe, 24.

Printed in the United States of America at
Corporate Graphics in North Mankato, Minnesota.

Table of Contents

Look at Us!

People are all different.

We are different shapes.

We are different sizes.

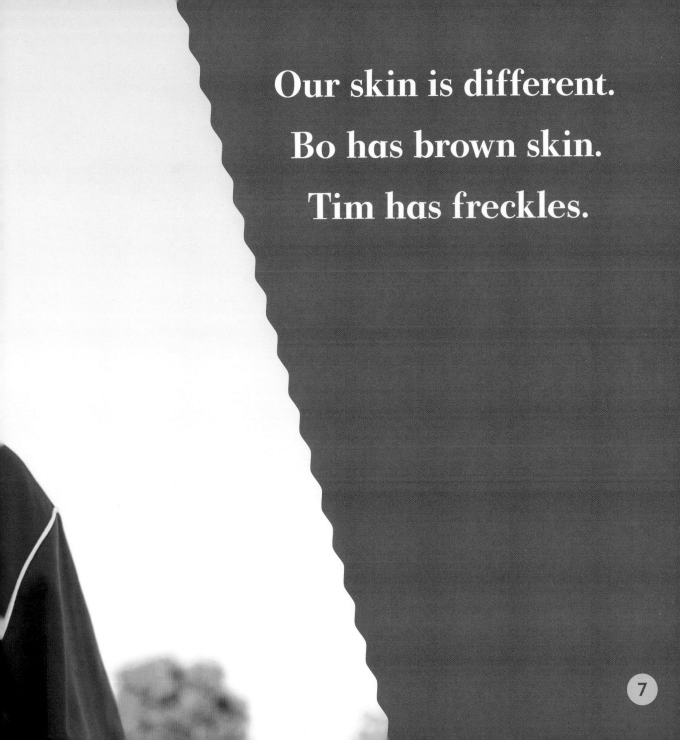

Our skin is different.
Bo has brown skin.
Tim has freckles.

7

Our hair
is different.

Min's hair
is straight.

Shay has curls.

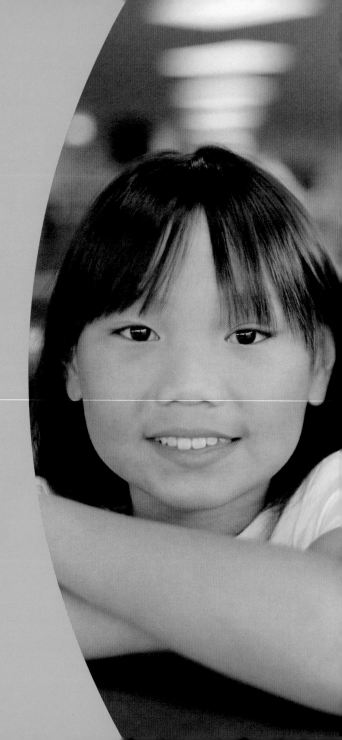

Meg has red hair.

Sami's hair is blonde.

glasses

We look different
in other ways, too.

Jack has glasses.

They help him see.

Erik has a wheelchair.
It helps him move.
Wow! He can really go!

wheelchair

braces ....

Look!

Dana has braces.

They straighten her teeth.

Clothes make us
look different, too.

Lila covers her head.

Avi wears a tall hat.

Look around you.

We are all different.

Each of us is unique.

Each of us is special!

Different Together

Look at all the ways **a group of friends can look** different from one another!

Picture Glossary

braces
Bands and wires that are put on the teeth to make them straight.

unique
One of a kind.

freckles
Brown spots on the skin.

wheelchair
A chair with wheels that people who cannot walk use to get around.

To Learn More

Learning more is as easy as 1, 2, 3.

1) Go to www.factsurfer.com

2) Enter "differentappearances" into the search box.

3) Click the "Surf" button to see a list of websites.

With factsurfer.com, finding more information is just a click away.